If This Were Real

If This Were Real

Gerda Stevenson

Published 2013 by
Smokestack Books
PO Box 408, Middlesbrough TS5 6WA
e-mail: info@smokestack-books.co.uk
www.smokestack-books.co.uk

If This Were Real
Gerda Stevenson
Cover image: Nina Rupena
Author photograph: Anna Wiraszka

Typeset by EPW Print & Design Ltd, Hartlepool.
Printed and bound in the U.K. by Biddles, part of the
MPG Books Group Ltd, Bodmin & King's Lynn.

ISBN 978-0-9571722-7-2

Smokestack Books is
represented by Inpress Ltd
www.inpressbooks.co.uk

for Aonghas, Rob and Galina,
and my parents,
always remembering Marsali.

Acknowledgements are due to the editors of the following magazines, newspapers and anthologies, where some of these poems were first published – *Aesthetica, Cencrastus, Chapman, Cork Literary Review, Down Syndrome Educational International, Edinburgh Review, The Eildon Tree, The Herald, Markings, New Writing Scotland, Parnassus: Poetry In Review* (New York), *The Scotsman, Spectrum magazine*; David Betteridge (ed) *A Rose Loupt Oot* (Smokestack Books), *Cleave* (Two Ravens Press), Judy Steel (ed) *Horse Tales and Saddle Songs* (Riding for the Disabled), *Wilderness* (Scottish Borders Council); 'Wartime Skipping Song' was written for *Pentlands At War* (Scottish Borders Council). Ten of these poems were included in *Invisible Particles*, a poetry pamphlet by Gerda Stevenson.

Special thanks to Catherine Lockerbie who, as Literary Editor of the Scotsman, first published my poetry, and to Tom Bryan, who, as Writer in Residence at Scottish Borders Council, asked me to write a poetry pamphlet, and got it published. I am also deeply grateful to the late Philip Hobsbaum, who encouraged me to keep writing, and, like Tom, wrote to the Scottish Arts Council (now Creative Scotland) in support of my work. Thanks to all the editors of newspapers, magazines and anthologies who have published my poetry, to my colleagues in The Pentlands Writers' Group – particularly Anita John – to Neil Astley, Morris Kahn, Carol K. Mack, Stuart Paterson, Goran Simic, Ronald and Marjorie Stevenson, and especially to Meg Bateman and Aonghas MacNeacail, for their invaluable feedback and encouragement.

Contents

Prelude

Storm at Carlin's Loup Rock

Winter's black hand
whips my hair
into a sudden tree.
'Dance or die!'
skirl the real ones,
and my feet itch
down the path
to the early bus.

'Night Speed' glares
a bulb-spangled truck
and is gone.

I stand like a stone,
let sky, wind and rain press
the weight of their season
into my skin.

No sign of my bus yet,
but Cutty Sark's in the air,
her breath on my neck.

Rather than travel,
I'd fling her my hand,
sink time in a whirlpool
and Strip the Willow
round Carlin's Loup.

Carlin's Loup, in folk etymology, means Witch's Leap

Part I: Eden

Eden

Bees cruised
on a breathless noon,
cabbage white butterflies
flickered in the lane.
Our dolls' china tea set
cracked the silence as we crept
over the neighbour's dyke,
spread a picnic under the rhubarb,
and stripped to our pink Scots skin.
We screeched and whooped
among the tall red stalks, striped
by their shadows in war paint glow,
squealed at the slap of leafy parasols,
shrieked as caterpillars fell to our knees
from pin-holes of light where they grazed.

Heels and stick
click down the path,
fingernail flames rip
through leaves: *'Get out!*
Get out of my garden,
you dirty, dirty girls!'

Snowberries

A milky way of marshmallow stars,
Snow Queen's fruit to tempt us,
though we knew never to eat them:
poison – even in their silent breath,
we thought – so we'd cup our hands
over mouth and nose, hardly dare
to inhale, crouched beneath
the lethal galaxy, thrilled
by death's proximity.

Butterflies

for Goran Simic

'I can't write about butterflies,'
laughed the war-torn poet,
corpses hanging from his every line.

And I remembered those wings
from childhood, shown by a neighbour,
rows of them, pinned behind glass,
frozen in a dream of flight,
intricate structures of weightlessness
that once rode the wind,
painting summer skies
in yellow, indigo and vermillion.

Then she took out a biscuit tin,
this same neighbour, showed me photos
from the war: Birmingham bombed;
a jaunty snapshot of her pilot husband
who went down with his plane, she told me,
and a newspaper cutting of naked bodies
piled high in a ditch at Belsen,
baking in the noon heat,
birch woods nearby, bright flecks
among the branches that might,
I thought, be butterflies.

Maggie Mowbray

Black you wore,
a sheen of grease
on your hair and coat,
a phantom to me, as I hid,
knee high at the garden gate,
one eye on the journey you made
each day from home to shop,
and home again,
string bag in hand,
black dog at heel.

Your back's bulk
gave me space
to snatch breath
while you locked up;
then you'd thrust your brow
at the world and its spies,
knuckles wrapped round the key
you'd lay with ritual precision
under a secret stone in the wall;
I'd wait for the scent of decay in your wake
as you shuffled off past me down the lane
for corned beef, milk and oranges.

On the day you died,
your dog was found dead
in its sideboard tomb.

A car fills your house now,
just enough room at its gleaming flanks
for deck chairs, parasol, lawn-mower and pram;
your walls sport a white-wash
I slapped on with pals
for our first teenage party;
not a ghost of you in our laughter,
as we scalloped the crepe-paper bunting
that trails a faded rainbow
round your one remaining window.

Head Master, Primary School

You knew it was coming:
snake eyes narrowed
to even thinner slits,
the jowls' habitual twitch
grew to fish gill gulps:
'Come out here – NOW!'

It was the meek ones he went for,
mild boys whose pale cheeks flushed
the moment his tongue lashed the stale air.
Floorboards girned as heels dragged
towards the spot. 'Now we'll see
what you're made of!' he'd boom,
sliding open the desk drawer,
releasing the tawse from its coiled coma,
stroking its grudge into action.
'Hold up your hands – HIGHER!'

And we'd watch the spasm
at each strike,
small shoulders braced
against the mortification of tears.

My Father's Chair

The Irish upholsterer
had the measure of it –
the ranks of roundhead tacks
hammered along its contours
still in place; a breathing pelt
in the music room's curtained murk
before piano keys release the day,
grey as morning smoke
spiralling from the grate,
silver rimmed when winter light
filters through fern frost,
redolence of Havana at the head-rest,
arms polished to a sheen with wear,
every fibre alive with tales he told us there,
and steeped in Bach's compassion.

Long ago, when work
had taken him far away,
I curled up in its belly
hearing him play
Song of the Traveller,
his unmistakable *parlando* tone
I knew even then floating
from another world that held him
in the Bakelite radio's glow.

Song of the Traveller/Chant du Voyageur, by Paderewski.

Linton Power Cut

The wires were aa doon wi the blizzard's virr,
black wicks stitterin intae life ahint
ilka door an frostit winnock, the lenth
o the snaw-happed street. The wind drapped and sooched
a dwaiblie braith, taigelt o the day's fecht;
the Gifford clock's greetin face wis steekit
at twenty past seeven, when the news swyped
the stern-lichtit lift: 'A lorry's skytit
and tummelt its load – oranges bleezin
doon the brae, gowd frae Seville in the snaw!'

Great Aunt Anne

We stepped from the cobbled street
straight into her parlour. Plaster saints
gleamed from cabinet grottos,
Windolene nipped our nostrils.
'Coom in! Cooom in!'
she called from the back room,
voice pitched to combat
half a century's clatter
of Lancashire looms,
each elastic syllable stretched
and shaped for clarity:
'Eee, me lumbaaaygo –
it's right bad todaaay,'
patting the pain,
that old familiar partner,
while she rocked by a frugal fire,
the air chilled as the flagstones.

Round her ears and brow
an immaculate plait coiled
like mill smoke, a frame
for her shammy-leather face.
That gypsy brown skin
made perfect sense of her name
to a child: Anne Tan;
great maiden aunt, elder sister of a brood,
the one who had to look out for the others
on pay-day night, when Mother
herded them through the back door
to huddle in a field among sheep,
till drunken Dad had done his worst
and was safely bedded, snoring.

'Sit nice, now,' she winked at us,
eyes like flints that sparked a smile,
and didn't miss a trick. 'Priest's cummin by.
He'd like to see you Scotch childer.'
A black cassock slid into the room –
on cue, as if she'd conjured it.

Suddenly she was a girl again,
muted in the patrician presence,
modest in making her introductions,
privileged to hand her scrimped pittance
into his outstretched palm.

The Catwalk

'Take care round this bend,'
warned our father, always,
at sight of the tallest pine.
'Single file!'
And the dolls' china tea-set
chinked in its basket,
as our toes detected
culprit roots
on the Catwalk path
above the gorge.
'Remember *those* sisters.'

I'd picture their eyes,
like the startled stars
of forget-me-nots
that grow on the bank
above the spot
where they tripped –
their dresses as blue –
and plunged
hand in hand
in the heedless 20's
through careless arms
of hazel and birch,
feet fluttering
a desperate Charleston
they'd never dance.

The Red Cardigan

I watched it grow on her needles
each night – moss stitch and rib,
a red rug sprouting wings.
One day it settled on her shoulders,
criss-crossed over her neat breasts
and held the wine glass stem of her waist
in a bright-buttoned hug.
She knocked that woman
on the knitting pattern page
into a cocked hat, not to mention
all the other mothers the length
of Main Street: she was Greta Garbo,
Gracie Fields and Ingrid Bergman,
all rolled into one. Even when it went
at the elbows, it was still a class act,
invisible darning an art in her hands –
you couldn't detect the seamless
transition from old to new.

It arrived, years on, out of the blue,
with her words: 'Your colour,'
and proved a perfect fit. I posed
in the mirror, checked every angle,
went out in it – once or twice;
but it was nothing without her grace
and I never looked the part.

First Love

'Let's walk,' he said, 'down that line of trees,'
so they left the road, and the field swayed
its seed-laden skirt, blood on the hem
from a low-spilling sun,
no words while they walked,
but a pleating of fingers,
the clamour of ravens' call in their ears.

'Take the bus,' he said, 'to my student room,'
so in after-school dusk, she left the wind-scoured
hills of home, and pressed a hot cheek
to the shuddering glass, cool balm
through the long miles in December's gloom.

Rasp of gear-change, wheeze of brakes,
and she steps at last into Edinburgh's shroud;
kirk spires dissolve, looming street-lamps
lead her on (virgin footsteps voiceless now
in the veiled air), and there's no going back,
past the college gate he enters each day,
down a cobbled lane to the winding well
of the tenement stair,
the cauldron she climbs
to his door.

'A cold night for it!'
the landlady croons,
casting her judgement
from the banister above,
linoleum glare and Calvin's zeal
glistening in a covert glance.

Moonlight and sleet on the windowsill;
the clock-tower tolls its tale of the last bus,
long gone, long gone.

Arm in arm,
out onto the landing,
they carol the night,
down through the stairwell,
into the street: Holly and Ivy,
The First Noel, Lo! A Star,
and foot it back, home to the hills
in the frosted air.

Part II: That Time Again

Co-op Funeral Parlour

My heart stops
at the waxed apple cheeks, plump
and impossibly polished;
your head in my palm yesterday,
skull barely masked by paper skin,
you were undeniably mine.
An imposter lies in this small white box
we ordered – a collector's doll,
lace-framed face mounted
on a slice of shop-window silk.
I would strip the pinned folds, find
the miracle of your miniature hands,
blood cooled to blue beneath each nail,
but a tail of brown thread,
carelessly trimmed, curls
below the jaw's angle, like a worm
emerging from puckered skin.
I draw back, let panic drain,
search for signs of you,
and detect at last
the down-turn of your top lip –
my mouth's copy –
under a lipstick blur.

Two Horses against a Hill

Two horses against a hill,
shoulder to shoulder,
one faces East, the other West,
and I think of us –
how we can be,
sometimes, at our best:
opposites, yet close enough
to cradle each other's different worlds
in a wide arc of peripheral vision.

Syndrome

3am, and a globe of the world
illuminates your sleep.
Pentland rain beats on the slates
above your head.

I saw you first on a screen –
sound brought you to light,
the curve of your brow
a distant moon; I knew
there was a chance
of that one chromosome.

I spin the globe
on its plastic axis,
oceans and continents
flicker over your face;
from the delicate slant of your eyelids
I'd guess Siberia or Tibet
if I didn't know.
Like that butterfly in China
your breath taps the air,
and shells strung for your delight
shift slightly on their threads.

You fill a space too small
to pin-point on the map,
but your territories are vast,
unfolding before me
a unique identity.

Gardening with Galina

Every word we've planted,
you and I, has been
so slow to grow,
each a seed bedded deep
in your mind's loam.
In the silence, we've waited,
as the seasons change, and meantime
learned that hands can speak;
until, at last,
shoots of green sound reach
from roots through your throat's reed,
leaves unfurl, spilling sunflowers from your lips:
dark seeds wreathed in gold for us to sow,
more and more golden words for us to grow.

The Lull

I look up from my book
to blossoms on the gean,
banked like snow above me,
glad of a lull
in the trunk road traffic –
only birdsong and bees in the air.

I close my book,
lay it on the bench,
and slip into my heart's road,
hoping for a lull there too,
that you might have fallen,
like the blossoms will,
but glad, in truth,
to find you rooted still.

Child in the Woods

You dip from sight
behind dark pines
on a steep bend
in the glen's well.

I wait, as always,
while you catch up,
listen for your answer
to my call,
for a stick's crack,
a stone's fall;
I'm a deer or dog, all
ears for you.

Then, at last, the signal sounds:
your new yellow mouth organ
threads the air in plaintive strains,
your white face rises over the ridge,
small moon cradled in low-slung boughs,
and my love rises at the gift of you.

Picking Chanterelles

Eyes bright with the search,
you clutch your small basket
under gusting silver birch,
summer's last flush on your cheeks;
and suddenly our luck's in –
a blaze of tiny can-can skirts
kick their hems at our feet.

Your pink fingernails plunge
their pocket-money glamour
into wet moss, your laughter
gold as the fluted flesh
you pluck from the earth.

The Visit

At the bend in the burn
where great beeches hang
in day's late light
you came to me
your stillness
immense.

Sky's membrane
your skin
sleep of sap
your blood.

If I move
or breathe
I'll lose
this touch I know
through years
of lack
is yours.

Passing Through

On a mellow spring morning,
hand in hand, my father and daughter –
one slowing down, one growing faster,
but today, stepping perfectly in time –
take a short-cut to the swing park
through the village grave-yard,
where snowdrops gleam, white
and still as the bones beneath.

And they linger a little, playing hide-and-seek
among faded tributes on lichened stones,
as they make their way from gate to gate
in the bright sunshine of another year.

Rob's Rap

Willow-limbed lad
with the peat-brown curls,
willow-limbed lad
with the sea-blue eyes,
willow-limbed lad
of the piping fingers,
silver songs
and dancing mind,
willow-limbed lad
of hungry questions,
you're the one for me.

Willow-limbed lad
of the concrete hair gel,
sleek-wheeled skate board,
dream-driven race track,
willow-limbed lad
of a thousand decibels,
growling, soaring bass guitar,
willow-limbed lad,
tender, remorseful,
willow-limbed lad,
searching, craving,
willow-limbed lad,
turning from me,
new roads in your gaze.

Thirteen now, and
you're nearly a man,
willow-limbed lad
of mighty opinions,
a million longings,
and impossible dreams,
willow-limbed lad
striding from me,
willow-limbed lad
on the far horizon,
willow-limbed lad
I'm watching, willing
my willow-limbed lad
as he dips from view.

Fiddler's Delight

for my niece Anna-Wendy Stevenson, in celebration of her composition 'My Edinburgh'

Girl with the red rose
that blooms in the lee
of your flaxen hair,
fiddle on shoulder, bow in hand,
ready now to lead the band
through streets strung
with your lilting notes,
each one a streaming lamp,
bright as all that Leerie lit;
your toe taps a bar,
your wrist whips
horse hair to cat-gut –
and we're off!

You jig and jaunt us
down cobbled closes,
snake us up stone stair-cases,
run us round the ragged rocks
to the languid lochs of Holyrood –
and back again; we strut with you
the Playfair pavements, Lairds
of the New Town for a while,
till the cello lurches, and drum beats
the sweat, hops and grime of Grove Street.

From brewery gutter to grey sky,
we soar high on a saxophone's wing,
then slide down a steep sigh,
while ivories ring the milk cart's clink
in another century's morning.

Then it's thrum, thrum,
the fiddle vamps,
the mandolin is finger-picking
and we're heel-clicking
past weans and tramps,
by geans in bloom –
Middle Meadow's long haul
to the top of the Walk,
through pulsing tone of traffic lights,
the last leg, the final fling
to Sandy Bell's – the doors swing
us into the bar, clatter and whoop,
we'll tak a stoup to the lass
that led us a canty dance,
and slake our drouth
at the well with her,
the quaich of airs still to sup.

*Sandy Bell's – the Edinburgh pub, home of world
renowned folk music.*

Your First Visit to Church

We booked a room
at an inn for the night,
and strolled by dusk
in holiday frocks
through a graveyard.
The moon lay low
on her slender back,
and yew trees in stately black
presided over a path to the door.
'Can we go in?' you asked,
and we found it open.

You strode up the aisle alone,
unafraid of the hushed gloom,
stained glass glint from the West
on your shoulders, and you paused
in the chancel, slim silhouette
against the wide East window,
child in a field of dwindling light,
listening, it seemed, to the silence.

'What do you think a church is for?'
I asked, curious, as we left.
'Singing,' came your answer,
quick and sure, 'for singing.'

My Son Stepping Out

My eye draws every line of you,
from the roots of your John Lennon mane
to the tips of your toe-tapping feet,
dressed for the high school ball
in your Grandad's white tuxedo.

The season's first snowflake
alights on your cheek as you
throw us a wave at the gate.

I tell you this,
and no mistake:
were I a girl again
on the dance floor tonight –
I know which choice I'd make.

How to Tell Him

on receiving news of my mother-in-law's death

I replace the phone on its cradle,
the news resting in my ear.
How to bring it to my mouth,
be midwife to words that will cut
the cord of their braided years?
How to tell him?

He looks up from his paper
like a child over a garden hedge –
her fond and only prodigal.
I can hear the clock on her mantelpiece
two hundred miles away, its tick
a pulse to the music of her days:
the hens' muffled clucking at her kitchen door,
the hot water tank's bubble and slurp
as the peat-blaze sears the back boiler;
the ferry's boom at the pier head,
the wind's whine up the croft brae.

She's still alive until I tell him,
sending eggs next week, as usual,
swaddling each fragile oval
in the *Press & Journal*'s folds;
tomorrow's pot roast is on the stove,
homage to the Sabbath, when
duty-bound, she'll take her ease;
and she's skinning Golden Wonders,
scooping salt herring from a plastic pail,
their scaled bellies a rainbow in her palm –
until I tell him.

Autumn Night

Leaves wheel at me out of the black
and skitter across pale sheets
that sigh on the line like tired lungs;
the pup tosses a stray quince
in the cold dew, while sweet steam rises
from the ones that reached the pot,
my mother a stooped blur
behind her kitchen window
as she stirs another year's harvest.

At Cille Choirill Church

We climbed again to Cille Choirill,
once the hill of sacred fire, high
above Glen Spean, golden birches
hushed sentinels in the still afternoon.
You ran over mossy mounds
where the dead lay, your red shift a pulse
among headstones twice your height,
voice piping a litany of MacDonalds:
Alexander, Isabella, Duncan, Hugh,
Angus, Donald, Kate, John – husbands, wives,
daughters, sons, a shoe-maker, a bard,
men accidentally drowned,
others killed in the Great War.
'Did they have arrows in their bellies?'
you called to me, wanting the hard facts.
'Bullets, probably,' I replied, absorbed
in lichened abstracts of older stones,
the mason's hand long obliterated.

Cille Choirill is pronounced Keela Chorrill, the 'ch' as in 'loch.'

My Father's Window

I walk down the street,
and see him,
framed behind glass,
grey head bowed
among his books.
All morning
he'll leaf the pages
of great men's lives,
and toast them at noon
with a savoured dram.
The air will be *dolce pianissimo*
with the nectar of sharing,
comparing notes
on keyboard mastery.

As the day wears on,
he'll leave them for a while
arrayed around the Steinway,
sepia shadows,
cravatted and coat-tailed,
awaiting his return
from post-lunch rest.
Restored, he'll enter
to their roar of mute applause,
take the platform and blaze
in the low winter light.

Birch Trees

My love like the green
of new birch leaves
after long sleep
awakened today
with your step
through the door.

Time in our skin now,
but the years fall away,
your touch young leaves
on bending boughs
of the old birch tree.

Year in, Year out

for Jenny

Year in, year out,
it sat on the stone beach,
just another rock, we thought,
the first time, till a gust
slipped under a loose flap,
and we saw it: ample back
and slumped seat –
the armchair, basking.

Year in, year out, sentinel
in storms we never weathered,
there for us, in sun and bluster,
as we scavenged for driftwood,
our broods clamouring
to be crowned on the throne,
tumbling over its beached bulk,
bleached plastic slapping
at its salt-cracked legs.

And year in, year out,
while the rowan on the shore
stretched like the children,
the armchair split – spine,
ribs and shoulders
a harp for the wind's play.

Year in, year out, until the day
we beach-combed and burned
its last stray bones,
as the berries blazed in the blue.

Time and Space

The full moon
pins us in its circle
as we meet
in the kitchen hallway,
each on some small
domestic mission.

I turn off the light,
the better to see us,
husband and wife,
held between walls
by the night's pure beam,
the journey we've made
through decades
to this moment,
a mere blink
of that cold eye.

Edinburgh Waverley

my parents still travelling

She's wearing her powder-blue suit
for the journey; its shade echoes her veins.
He's dapper, though stooped,
in his light summer jacket,
shadow of a dashing man;
'I prefer the quiet nowadays,'
he sighs at the station's dissonance.

I leave them on the platform,
with time in hand, satisfied now
they're no longer fretting
over daily medication,
location of passports,
quantity of kroner,
settled and prepared
for what's to come.

As I drive away,
I see them in my wing mirror,
standing side by side,
waiting for their train to draw in.

That Time Again

for Marsali, 5.2.81–15.2.81

In down-at-heel, forgotten
Kinning Park, an angel's wings
pierce the winter sky;
rooftop relic of another day,
she stands in stubborn splendour,
stone quills poised
in one perpetual instant.

The heaving road beneath her
rumbles West, by building sites,
bridging Clyde, past fields,
through moors, by mountains,
Cruachan's peaks, to loch-side,
moss and bed of earth,
where (was it moments, years
or even those two decades back?)
we placed you.

That time again,
that time of year,
and every white-legged lass
in Kinning Park today
to my keen eye
has angel shadows
in her glance, the look,
the possibility of you.

Wedding Anniversary

Heading South from Larne to Kerry,
I like to think I'm in the driving seat,
but you're the world's worst navigator,
reading the map, yes, though not the route,
relishing the place names, every Gaelic road sign
guessing their meanings, leading us astray
by Baile Atha Fhirdhia – Town of the Ford
of the Man of God, on past An Uaimh –
The Cave, through An Chulchoill –
The Back Woods, while Cnoc an Tochair –
Hill of the Dowry, beckons from the East;

the two of us, today, fording another stretch of time,
though we're not of that god, the one of the black book –
we belong to one whose work is all around us here
in Cluain Meala – Field of the Honey, on this mellow
midsummer's eve, three decades since we tied the knot,
taking ages, forever, it seems, to reach An Coirean –
The Pool, because the words beguile you
from the straight and narrow, as they've always done,
my dear, mo charaid, mo ghraidh, leading us to places
I might never have seen, places that are mapped now,
forever, on my tongue and in my heart.

Father-minding

Your piano keys
don't ripple the air today –
you're tired, you say,
so we sit together, quiet;
it's what you want –
you need your rest
and take it.

The faulty smoke alarm's erratic bleep
from somewhere upstairs doesn't trouble you,
nor a dog's insistent bark far down the street;
and the sudden clatter of unseasonable hail
on the darkening window is of no concern;
the book on your knee lies open,
pages fanning from the spine
as your fingers relax their grip;

outside, bunting flaps its frantic dance,
reclaiming last week's annual fling,
a silent film that runs and runs
behind the still life
of you.

Shirt

You slipped from our bed before dawn,
to catch an early flight. Mid-morning,
I pick up your shirt from the laundry pile,
bury my face in the tang of you - rehearsal,
perhaps, for a time when you won't return;

I stand in our bedroom, clutching that cloth,
your possessions ranked about me,
benign for once, not the dead weight
of their crowded ballast drowning me as usual,
daylight's sheen blessing their contours,
so bright I could cry at their frailty,
orphans adrift;

no compass now, the needle astray, loose
in its housing, mocking the daily degrees
of rage that suddenly count for nothing,
all points blurred into one without you,
no direction, no way to measure, no map,
no fine distinctions, no True
or Magnetic North.

Part III: Reading the Tree

Wartime Skipping Rhyme

Cellani and Lenati,
the braw Italianati,
POWs
doon in Robinsland Farm.

Cellani and Lenati,
nae mair speghatti,
they miss their Tally grub
doon in Robinsland Farm.

Cellani and Lenati
diggin the potati,
they're fryin up chips
doon in Robinsland Farm.

Cellani and Lenati
say we're daft as a banani,
they're great for a laugh
doon in Robinsland Farm.

Cellani and Lenati
dinnae drive a Bughatti
but they gie tractor rides
doon in Robinsland Farm.

Cellani and Lenati
brew rosehip Frascati,
we're gonnae hae a party
doon in Robinsland Farm!

Cellani and Lenati
Cellani and Lenati
Braw Italianati,
Braw Italianati

Lenati's in la notte
speakin sotto voce
Mary's in her nightie
in the braw moonlightie
Lenati and his lassie
doon in Robinsland Farm.

Mary and Lenati,
bye-bye, ma bonnie birdie,
Mary and Lenati,
so long, arrivaderci,
Mary and Lenati,
triste, triste,
Mary, lassie, Mary,
forget aboot Lenati,
Mary, lassie, Mary,
mind on Mussolini,
ye cannae love Fascisti
cut yer losses, lassie –
leave.

Homework for Evacuee Day

We select ten objects, things you'd pack,
if this were real; and you place them,
(with all the care you sense they're due
from all you've learned on the matter),
in a child's old-fashioned suitcase –
the one I carried in a play about a war –
the kind we'd give you,
if you were leaving us for safety,
if now were then, and this were real:
a skipping rope, its arc in the air
a last fling before we wind it tight –
a yellow mouth organ waiting
for your breath; a book
whose story will feed you every night,
though you'll have to read yourself to sleep,
and your tattered, one-eyed mermaid,
nocturnal swimmer by your side, soon
to be beached on unfamiliar sheets;
a ball of wool skewered with needles,
to make the scarf we started,
if you can remember *in, over, through, off*
without my prompt; pencil and paper
to tell us of your days, and a box of dominoes
'to count them,' I say;
a photo of us all, arms linked,
laughing under autumn apples
'before the first bomb fell,' you say,
as if what's happening is real,
and you really have to go.

View from a Plane

I'm part of the air,
steel ribs encase me,
and sipping tea,
I view night's carpet
networked in needlepoint.

Flying from my son –
perhaps I'm vapour trail in his mind
as he's strapped into his capsule,
driven home at his father's side
through glowing strings of sodium.

I leaf through newsprint,
drain my cup, lulled
by turbine hum;
'Bomb attack in school,
children slaughtered
at their desks.'
I fold the news away.

Manchester below,
or Birmingham,
but I see Sarajevo,
all her cables cut,
where a candle stump
in a father's fist spits its path
through rubble, and spots
the trail of children's brains
smeared on schoolbook pages.

Reading the Tree

in memoriam Ferida Osmanovic, Tuzla, July 1995

At first he thought she was reading the tree,
her face so close to its bark –
initials and an arrow through a heart, perhaps,
love's declaration to the world?
Chin poised in concentration,
right-angled to her spine,
she stands so long it must be a book,
a tale with as many circles as trees have rings.
Morning sunlight slants down her back,
her red cardigan a still flag,
white cotton skirt among green leaves
proof of summer. He follows the line
from calf to ankle, her bare feet relaxed
above the forest floor, toes
testing the air in gentle levitation.
A distant wail of women lifts his eye
to the tell-tale plaited belt and shawl,
fatal collar of her own design.

Should he focus the lens, click
his shutter on the image,
though the news-desk may refuse it,
expose the moment's privacy,
delicate as the spider's web suspended
between twigs at his temple,
the extremity she chose, this woman,
whose faith in the blue helmets,
he will be told, dissolved at the locked gates,
whose husband, he'll learn, made sad guitars
from scrap wood to keep them fed, the man
she could not believe would never return
when the men with guns took him,
the mother, whose children
from this day on, will read in all trees
the strange fruit he is about to frame?

*After the photo by Darko Bandic. Ferida's husband was
murdered in Srebrenica. His body was never found.*

Last Bus Ride in July

July, 1995 - Genocide, Srebrenica
July, 2008 - Karadzic captured, Belgrade

Summer grass is shoulder high once more,
higher than my sons will ever be.
How could it grow again after what it saw?
Did its million seed-head eyes close tight
on next year's crop, at the first scent of blood?
Didn't it see what I saw, the jerk
of young shoulder blades, naked as plucked wings
at the gun barrels' thrust? I'd felt those bones
slide from my hips like baby clam shells
to their estuary of light – that push you knew
would be the last – once the shoulders were out –
the rest was easy.

But July has been a hard birth every year –
his shadow stalking the calendar, that man,
still out there, somewhere, breathing –
since the day those buses growled,
hungry to fill their bellies for the death run,
bus-load after bus-load of wrist-bound sons,
brothers, husbands, frail old grandfathers weeping
through glaucoma clouds, filing past the laden plum trees –
how could they bloom and fruit again,
those branches, drop their blind eyes
at my feet? As if I could ever make sweetness in July,
that month when pollen on the breeze will always
be the stench of fear and petrol fumes;
when the football field's mown grass reeked
of blood, July that tips the year's balance, knives
in its cry so sharp they cut summer's artery and bleed us
straight into winter;

until today, today, when July held its breath,
and winked to another hungry bus, just one
this time, that grumbled through Belgrade
on its peacetime daily run, wheezed to a halt
and swallowed the morsel he'd become, the man
whose shoulders once banked high as thunder clouds
above us, draped in that black gangster coat,
dressed for the opera, you'd have thought,
his coiffed plume cocked in obscene vanity.

And now the pollen has a hint of honey
in its stench; perhaps I'll try to cut the grass again,
smell its green juice instead of blood, pick the plums
and let my face sweat in their sweet condensation,
hold the jar to the light, and might
even taste the season's possibility.

Sarajevo Roses

General Ratko Mladic captured, May 2011

My wife says it's the roses,
not the house, the roses,
full-bodied blooms that grew
from a neighbour's cuttings,
back home in Srebrenica,
one for each of our three sons
when they were born – it's those roses
she'll never see again,
that tear her heart right out.

'Allah can't help you, but Mladic can!'
bragged the general, swaggering through
the crowded compound, flanked by his men,
dropping bread and coca cola into our palms
like manna from his own personal heaven -
next moment a gun at your head, flung
into trucks, pressed against strangers,
lungs scorched in the crush;

wheels rumble, fear riding the black night;
fear making my wrists sweat, till the rope
somehow slackens, and I jump, crawl
like a snake through the forest floor,
gunshots and shouts behind me, below me,
roving the air for my flesh.

And then
something good happened:
a bird sang; daylight came –
I could see, think, even hope,
and in the baking sun, my hair
brittle with dust and blood,
I reached safety,
but without them.

It's the roses, she says, not the house,
so she makes new ones,
where we're staying now,
gets down on her knees
in Sarajevo, and fills the scars
left by mortar shells – those eruptions
where the living fell –
fills them with blood-red resin,
strange blooms, whose petals may fade
but will never fall, pinned
to the street's breast.

Sarajevo Roses: throughout the city, scars from mortar explosions have been filled with red resin to mark where people were killed during the Bosnian War.

Ballad of the Sadr Carpenter

Once I made tables, chairs and beds,
but now it's coffins by the mile,
and wardrobes have another life –
barely emptied before they're filled –
far fewer married now than killed.

Once we had only two great rivers,
now a third: the Crimson Ditch,
where stray dogs lick the flooded banks,
the sweet-sour spate that sticks to our feet
in bone-dry rubble and dust-blown heat.

Once we had libraries and schools;
now scorpions swarm the cracked walls,
where blank-eyed orphans chant their lesson,
chalked on the board like a blessing:

the English words
for father, mother,
sister, brother,
family,
family,
family.

Girl in the News

Your eyes on the front page
snare me – a shy glance from Iraq.
Your lips curve the survivor's apology,
shoulders hunched by pressure of crutches,
the crater behind you once a street
that swallowed your left leg.

'Mute and deaf since birth,' says the news.
Did you watch the man in the market
selling songbirds blue as desert skies,
while clouds banked below the horizon
dark with the purr of hate?

Did your mouth shape a still-born scream
at the bombs and buildings that fell
without warning, silent as blossoms,
at the sudden jet of blood from your thigh,
at the soundless ambulance that swerved
into view too late for your family –
the only ones who knew how to speak
your lilting language of hands?

Saint Catherine

Remember me when the sun
arcs over your circling earth,
and the moon's belly grows to fullness.
I am the patron of your daughters,
of wheelwrights, poets and philosophers.
I never feared thought's labyrinth,
I gloried in the spirals of debate.
I led the Empress and her wise men
to conversion's light; I knew my worth,
and would not, could not have it thirled
to a witless master's chains.
The Emperor tried to break me on the wheel,
would have cracked my limbs
and laced them through the radials,
but my faith broke the wheel first.
He feared my mind, so split it
from its stem, and I watched my head,
just eighteen years and all that learning,
spin into the basket; milk spurted
from my veins, like the spitting stars
that spray from whirring silver discs
on black nights when bonfires blaze.

My bones, they say, were borne
on angels' wings to high Mount Sinai,
where the stone walls raised in my name
gave Christ's succour to Mohammed,
and still stand strong among the Bedouin,
a hub on the mountain pass, ringing praise
through time's wheel.

Santa Maria La Real

Siesta in Pamplona, and snow falls slow
as the cathedral gates begin to close.
Three blue pines, caged in the cloister's
lancet arches, reach for their square
of laden sky, and receive flake upon flake
with the same mute grace that Santa Maria
La Real accepts the chill of her silver robes
applied by the smith to her wooden flesh –
the carved Virgin of Navarre.

Silent, she rests at the city's heart,
a distant star in a cobalt dome,
remote from all show of devotion,
flanked by the royal tomb's
padlocked spikes – so high
on her throne we can only believe
in the subtle line of her painted cheek,
in the nestling infant on her knee.

A door booms through shadowed stone;
votive flames shudder in their corner shrine,
and lingering pilgrims steal a last glance
at the lone priestess, the miniature queen,
whose eyes catch mine from the postcard rack
on the way out. I make my purchase,
and study her features, as I step
into the snow-hushed street:
a peasant girl's quiet face,
under the load of a mighty crown;
no fear for the future marks her brow;
no trace in her gaze of the sad tale to come –
just the gentle certainty of breast milk.

Night Meeting

The pavement's a tightrope
she teeters along
in high-heeled patent leather,
the lamp posts like ropes that sway
from her grasp, as she lurches
from glow to glow;
a sudden halt, and she slumps
into the road's net,
baffled by its hard slap.

'Can I help?' I ask.
'Going home,' she pouts,
adjusting a strap in the trough
of her milk-white shoulder, then heaves
herself onto hands and knees,
and with one regal surge
evolves into the frosted night
from four legs to two.
'Home…' she sighs, as if
the word had lost its bearings.
'I'll chum you,' I offer,
gathering her strewn coat and bag.

We walk in silence along the street –
once an open road where I'd pick rosehips
with schoolmates for the National Health -
till she hauls us to a standstill: 'Oh, Christ!
Got to go back, back to the pub –
left the kids' Christmas presents.'
I steer her forward, no resistance,
'Get them tomorrow - there's still a week.'
'You one of those bloody Christians?'
'What makes you think that?'
'Must be, the way you're carrying on.'

At the corner, she stops:
'That's far enough –
he mustn't see me being helped home.
He'll kill me. Go on, Christian – scram!'

I watch till she dissolves
in the shadowed hallway
of her brand new house,
blue screen flicker
in its one open eye.

Christmas Market

Arms linked, eyes locked,
wreathed in each other's breath,
they sip mulled wine and kiss.

Is their love new, keen as the tang
of lemon rind, or old and warm
as cinnamon and cloves?
Whatever the vintage, they're held
in its circle tonight, anonymous
within the crowd's geometry, still hub
among the stalls' kaleidoscope.
Their bodies blend with intimate ease,
grey heads haloed by Ferris wheel neon,
oblivious to the caged cargoes
that shriek thrilled terror
into the Season of Love.

L'église Saint Michel

She stepped into silence
and closed the door
on her husband's rage.

Though blooms flamed
in the chilled gloom,
her heart's clamour stilled
in the mild presence
of Madonna and child;
till she read the names
on a marble plaque –
a litany of the city's sons
lost in the world's great rages.

Asylum Seeker

'From Damascus,' he told me,
'a military surgeon –
I couldn't perform
the punishment required:
couldn't cut off their ears.'
'Ears?'
'That's right,' he replied,
taking the rim of my own
between finger and thumb,
marking its curve to the lobe.
'Inhuman,' he said, 'I couldn't.'

His eyes hold the tale he
has to tell, cinnamon eyes,
and a smile spiced with loss.
'Your name,' he laughs softly,
'sounds like guard.
So it's hard for me to say.'

Months behind bars, and more
on the road; rain, snow,
ice, hail and heat,
borders and checkpoints,
gripping a chassis,
foetus folded
in the dark of a hold –
return to the womb,
though this one's cold.

Back in Damascus
wife and son gone to ground,
occasional phonecalls,
false name supplied,
while here in Glasgow,
where the daffodils shine,
this quiet surgeon with the delicate touch,

this quiet surgeon of the cinnamon eyes,
tells his tale, here in Glasgow,
where politicians' smiles
are spiced with lies,
their ears deaf to truth,
though still intact.

I am the *Esperance*

commemorating the Upper Clyde Shipbuilders' work-in

I am the *Esperance*, I sail in your wake,
canvas unfurled, bellied with hope
as you pour into Glasgow Green –
we are your chorus, my sisters and I,
your creation, a fleet of belief, heading back to the Clyde
from the seven seas: veteran *Hikitia*, floating crane,
the only one of her kind in the world, she's home again
from Wellington; and *Empire Nan*, our stout tug;
Delta Queen – her great stern wheel churns the foam
as she steams in from the Mississippi; and bold *Akasha*,
laden with memories of the Nile; we shimmer for you,
our riggings clink, our funnels boom to your cry:
'The Right To Work, Not a Yard Will Close,
Not a Man Down the Road,' your banners and flags
like waves before us, drawing us home in one great tide,
Umoja's here, her name bearing our purpose today –
unity – a gleam on her prow; *Moonstone* and *Seva*,
who well as any know all about salvage –
and there's *Uhuru*, named for freedom,
Uhuru, Uhuru, my sister *Uhuru*, sailing with me
in your wake, my canvas unfurled, freighted with hope,
as wave upon wave, you surge into Glasgow Green.

Part IV: Beyond Fairliehope

Fair Wind

An owl's cry
widens the night,
and my washing line
lengthens to the stars.
I'm poised, peg in hand,
to make the moment
last. Steam rises
from a fleet of sails,
becalmed in moonlight.
They'll be dry by morning,
given the fine forecast,
and a fair wind.

Nests

Black tree on white sky
in my windscreen,
soundtrack submerged
by engine hum, brakes
and gear-change.

A monochrome bird
arches into frame,
twig in beak tracing
line of flight,
sets its cargo
in the wayward arms
of a waltzing branch,
and is gone;
perfect timing,
no need to pause
for thought.

Sound as a stone
the twig remains,
slender linchpin,
dissolved only by distance
in my rear-view mirror.

Volcano in April

for Peter Cheeseman, who would not travel by air

There's no fast way to reach you
on the one day I need to,
planes all grounded, no fast way
to the place I need to be;
but you're laughing up your sleeve,
you, who had no truck
with silver service in the sky,
you're laughing now, before you die,
laughing with the birds you love
and took the time to learn –
the pitch of every call, curve
of beak and wing, the tailored cut
of every layered tail –
you're laughing with them
as they spin and swoop and tumble
in all that space, which, for once,
is how you'd have it, always.

Heron

Each day,
as we round
the river bend,
the dog and I,
we hope;

then watch
the steel grey silence
rise from the roar
of its waterfall haunt.

Kissing

Rain falls on the North Sea,
water kissing water, wave
after wave of salt tongues
licking their fill of clouds' spill.

The headland looks on
through the gathering veil –
an old woman
in bedrock tweed
who pays no heed
to the weather's discretion –
she's seen it all.

Catterline in Winter

after the painting by Joan Eardley

The houses are sledging
down the hill
in the blind gaze
of a pandrop moon.
Not a soul to be seen
in this battered landscape,
under a bullet-grey sky,
though someone's washing
hangs out in the damp;
perhaps they're asleep – a widow
or lovers behind a blue door,
dreaming of imperceptible slippage.

All lights out,
except for one,
its tilted frame
a well of yellow laughter,
beacon for travellers,
pulsing through wind-scoured scrub.

Director in Rehearsal

for Gerry

Within four walls
of a faded church hall,
you sense the moment,
and through your eyes
we glimpse its presence.

A truck rumbles past,
raising at least
a century's dust
to caper in shafts
of Leith's grey light,
where you are poised,
hearing only hooves,
the glittering hooves
of the hunt you lead,
and the nearing heart-beat
of its quarry.

To an Old Clown

'What's Art for?' people ask,
and I've asked myself the same.
But I'm glad, dear jester, jouster,
rowdy old clown, I'm glad
we dance and sing while earth spins,
even if the stories we tell
are just a fleck on time's stage –
that grand design of infinite entrances
and exits, with no horizons ever – glad
we don the daft motley, paint
our faces, and, at the very least,
make each other laugh;

though when new light shines
down years to come, who knows
who'll remember, and, if they do,
who'll understand the spot-lit lies,
floodlit truths, and shadowed ambiguities
in our retellings of the world's old tales?

Last Sunday

for Simon MacKenzie

Your skin glares yellow as lemon peel,
hairless head a bloated mask.
Only a wrist band confirms you're here,
till lips part, and in quiet Gaelic tones
you thank me for coming, ask for news
of my family. It seems like a taunt
to say we're well, so I tell you instead
my son has your language, passed
the exam with flying colours.
Mouth and eyelids flicker approval
as you fumble at nostrils to adjust
the oxygen's angle, pin cushion hand
sprouting wires. You lower its palm
into mine. We hold silence.

The hospice doors wheeze
to a close behind me.
A robin flits onto a litter bin.
Gulls wheel on spring gusts
to the clink of a bare flagpole.

The Honey Man

We ring a bell under the fig trees,
and wait. Crickets drill the July noon.
'*J'arrive! J'arrive!*' his frail voice pipes
from a hive of connecting chambers,
his slippered progress slow as the tortoise
that shifts towards a patch of shade
in its parched pen.

'Bonjour!' his waxen smile glimmers
from a dim interior, his form
a wrinkled husk in the half-light,
leading us through cool corridors
to his store. He selects a jar,
holds it up to a cracked window:
gold, laced by the sun's fractured rays.
'*Un miel delicieux, mademoiselle,*'
he promises, knuckles cradling
summer's labour, gleaned
from blue rosemary
in the high Pyrenees.

Fim

1988-2011

You were one syllable,
just one, the first consonant
a whisper, like your shyness,
giving quiet birth to the long vowel:
a gleam like your life, stretching
to the final exit, the last sound
lingering on closed lips
that can find no words
for such loss.

Planting Honeysuckle

I thought twice about it –
could be digging my own grave
under the electricity pole –
especially when I read the warning –
not the black zig-zag on the danger sign,
but a bird's skull in spring grass,
thin as the shell it broke through.

Could a spade's depth be enough?
Would the blade strike an old artery
wrapped in rust, but alive
to the prize of my flesh?

The Ballad of the Female Watchmaker

a tribute to playwright Lluisa Cunille

Time slips from these clocks
into my skin, and I cannot locate
the accumulation of seconds
within each pore.
The rusted face at my back
with no hands
gives ease to my mind,
which chases infinite flocks of divisions.

Like my father before me,
I order the hours, encase them in glass,
but still they seep through the rims
and fill my lungs, invisible particles
slowing my step.

In the room above,
childhood is locked
and rented out
to an unknown tenant,
whose breath stirs the air
as she passes my door,
ascending, descending,
ascending, descending,
not yet claiming
her right to remain.

Beyond Fairliehope

Last day of the old year,
and I cover the cake I've drip-fed
with brandy for weeks
(long since breached and complimented),
leave the fire well stoked –
safely guarded now – and close the door
on the churning circle of family need,
on the round of chores never complete.

Minus nine, and the sun's declining
as I tread the brittle path
through frosted hills to black pines,
the burn like the girl with ebony hair,
locked under a glass lid.

Still a fillet of sunlight on the brow above,
my goal to be splashed by those rays;
I know where the grouse will ambush me,
and I'm ready when its fear shrieks:
'Go back! Go back!'

Sweat down my spine,
thirst on my tongue,
heart a drum as I climb the brae
that once heaved into new birth
under a silent ice sheet –
reach the ridge,
and stand in the glow
of the year's last spark.